SECOND GRADE
Social Studies

SEMESTER B

ACCELERATE EDUCATION

Table of Contents

Module 19 1

Module 20 4

Module 21 7

Module 22 10

Module 23 16

Module 24 21

Module 25 27

Module 26 30

Module 27 36

Module 28 44

Module 29 48

Module 30 50

Module 31 55

Module 32 60

Module 33 65

Module 34 68

Module 35. 72

Module 36 76

Cutout Worksheets 83

This workbook contains all of the worksheets found in the
Social Studies 2 Semester B course. To see the worksheet in color, view it online
within the lessons. For any worksheets containing cutting activities, they can be
found in the "Cutout Worksheets" section.

© 2023 by Accelerate Education
Visit us on the Web at www.accelerate.education

Social Studies

Name: _____ Date: _____

Historical Questions

Each box below has a question about the past. **Choose two** questions to answer using the Internet. Type both questions in the search bar, one at a time. Write your answers on the lines below.

1. When did America become a country? _____ _____ _____	2. What state was the last state to join America? _____ _____ _____
3. Who was the first American woman in space? _____ _____ _____	4. Who invented potato chips? _____ _____ _____

19.1 Accessing Information

Social Studies

Name: _____ Date: _____

My Artifact

Think of one artifact that shows something important about the way you live, what you like, or what you believe. Draw a picture of that artifact in the box. Then answer the questions below.

My Artifact:

next page

1. Write one sentence to describe your artifact.

2. Write one sentence to explain what your artifact will tell future archaeologists about your life.

Social Studies

Name: _____ Date: _____

Changing Communication

Think about all the ways that people have communicated with one another over time. People share information faster now because of technology. In this activity, you will draw and write about communication.

1. In the box on the left, draw a picture of a type of communication used in the past. In the box on the right, draw a picture of a type of communication used in the present.

Communication in the Past	Communication in the Present

2. Describe how communication has changed over time and how technology has helped people communicate better.

_____
_____
_____
_____

20.1 Communication: Past and Present

Social Studies

Name: _____ Date: _____

Old and New Transportation

People have used vehicles for transportation for a long time. Technology has helped make transportation easier and faster. Use what you have learned to complete the activity below.

Directions:

1. Look at the pictures of the old transportation vehicles below. Write the name of each vehicle on the line under the picture.

2. Find the picture of the present-day transportation vehicle that replaced the old vehicle either online or in a magazine. Print it, cut it out, and paste it in the box.

3. Write a sentence that explains how technology has changed each type of transportation.

next page

5

20.2 Transportation: Past and Present

20.2 Transportation: Past and Present

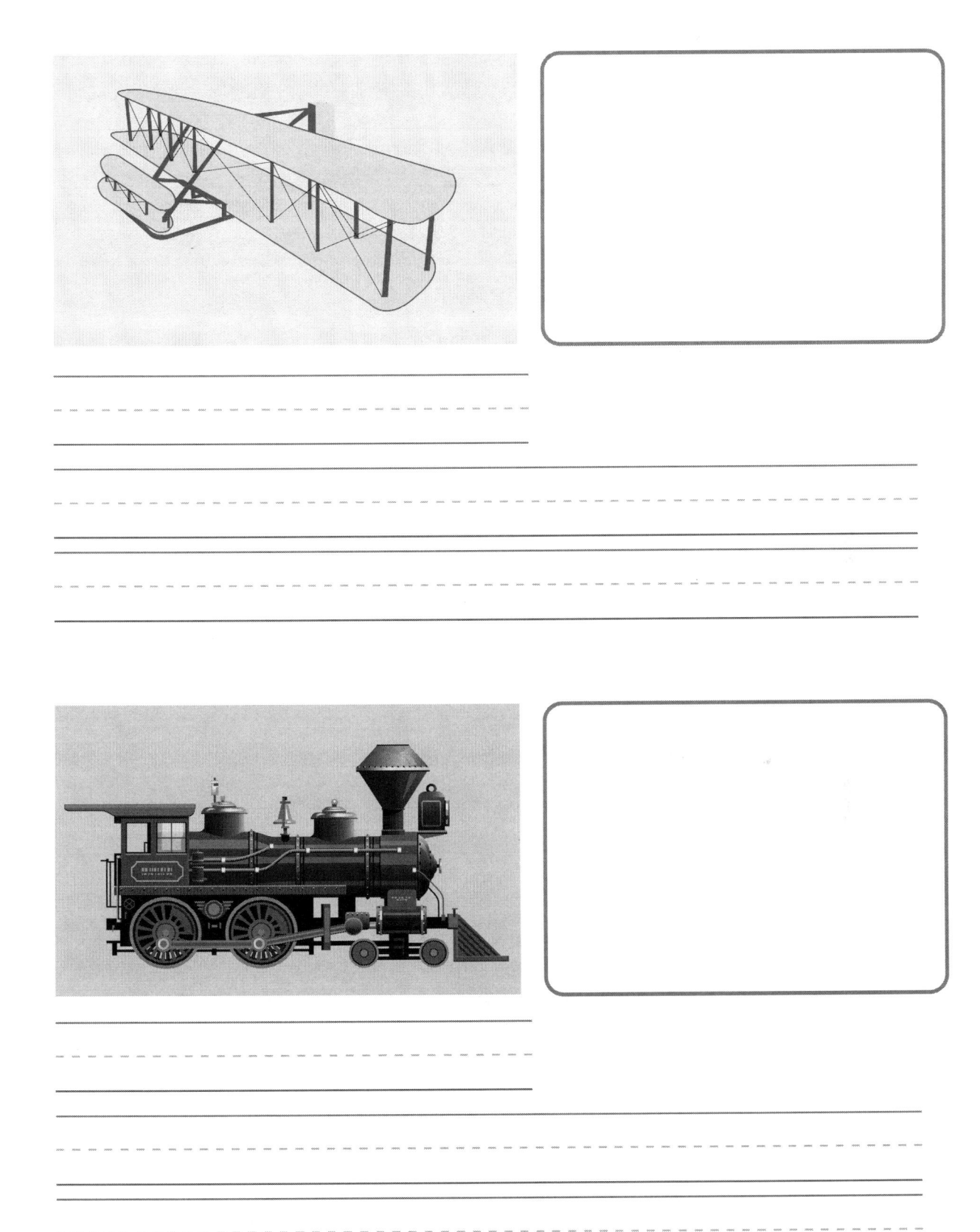

Social Studies

Name: _____ Date: _____

How Are My Basic Needs Met?

Technology and science help meet our basic needs every day. Look at the pictures below. Each one represents a basic need that we must have every day. How are these basic needs met with technology or science? Write your answer in complete sentences under each picture.

1.

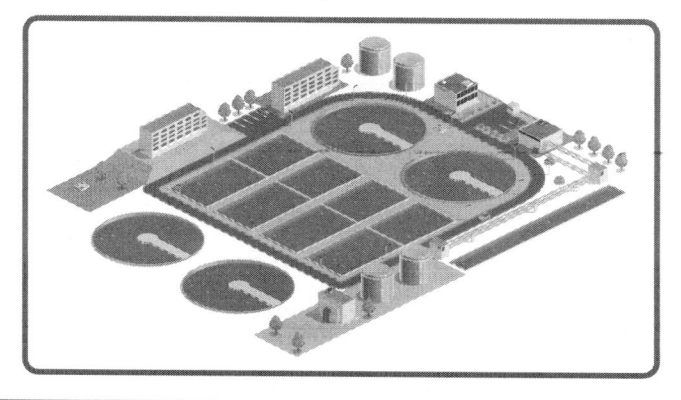

2.

7   21.1 Science and Technology Every Day

3.

4.

21.1 Science and Technology Every Day

Social Studies

Name: _____   Date: _____

My Own Invention

Do you have what it takes to be an inventor? Use what you have learned to complete the activity below. Think of your own invention that can help solve a real-life problem. Write down the problem in the **Problem** box. Next, create an invention that will solve that problem. Draw your invention in the **Invention** box. Then write a complete sentence to answer the question in the last box.

Problem	Invention

How does your invention solve the problem?

Social Studies

Name: _____ Date: _____

My Personal Story

Think about what you want your story to be about. Answer the questions below to help you plan your story.

1. Who are the characters in your story? List them below.
   _____
   _____
   _____
   _____
   _____

2. Where is the setting of your story? Write or draw the setting.

next page →

22.1 My Story

3. What happens at the beginning of your story? How does your story start?

4. What is the problem in your story? Is there a mystery, surprise, or big event?

5. What happens in the middle of your story to the characters?

6. What happens at the end of your story? How does the problem get solved?

next page

22.1 My Story

7. Use your planning sheet to write your personal story. Include the characters, setting, beginning, middle, and end. Be sure to add details! You can use a separate sheet of paper if you need more space to write.

22.1 My Story

Name: _____ Date: _____

Compare and Contrast

You will compare and contrast your personal story with an American hero's story. First, select an American hero's story from this lesson. Look for details from each story, and write them in the Venn diagram below.

1. Write the title of your story over one circle.
2. Write the name of the American hero you selected over the other circle.
3. Write details that are true only for your personal story in the circle for your story.
4. Write details that are true only for the American hero's story in the circle for the hero.
5. Write details that are the same for both stories in the middle section of the Venn diagram.

22.2 My Story in a Venn Diagram

Social Studies

Name: _____ Date: _____

My Different Perspective

The experiences you have can shape your perspective. Use what you have learned to complete the activity below.

1. Think of a chore you do not enjoy completing. Write about or draw a picture of that chore in the box below.

Chore:

next page →

17

23.2 Perspective of Experience

Social Studies

Name: _____ Date: _____

My Map Legend

Now it is your turn to create a map of your important places. Use the personal story you already wrote. Include a map legend that describes the icons that you will use on your map.

1. Follow the steps below to help you create your own map and legend.

Step 1: Write two locations to place on your map.
_____
_____
_____
_____

Step 2: Draw a picture for each location to create icons for your map legend.

Step 3: Write a description for each icon.
_____
_____
_____
_____
_____

next page →

22.3 My Story in a Map

14

2. Now, look at the map of the United States. Draw your pictures, or icons, on the map to show the locations that you identified in step 1. Then create a legend using the icons and descriptions you created in steps 2 and 3.

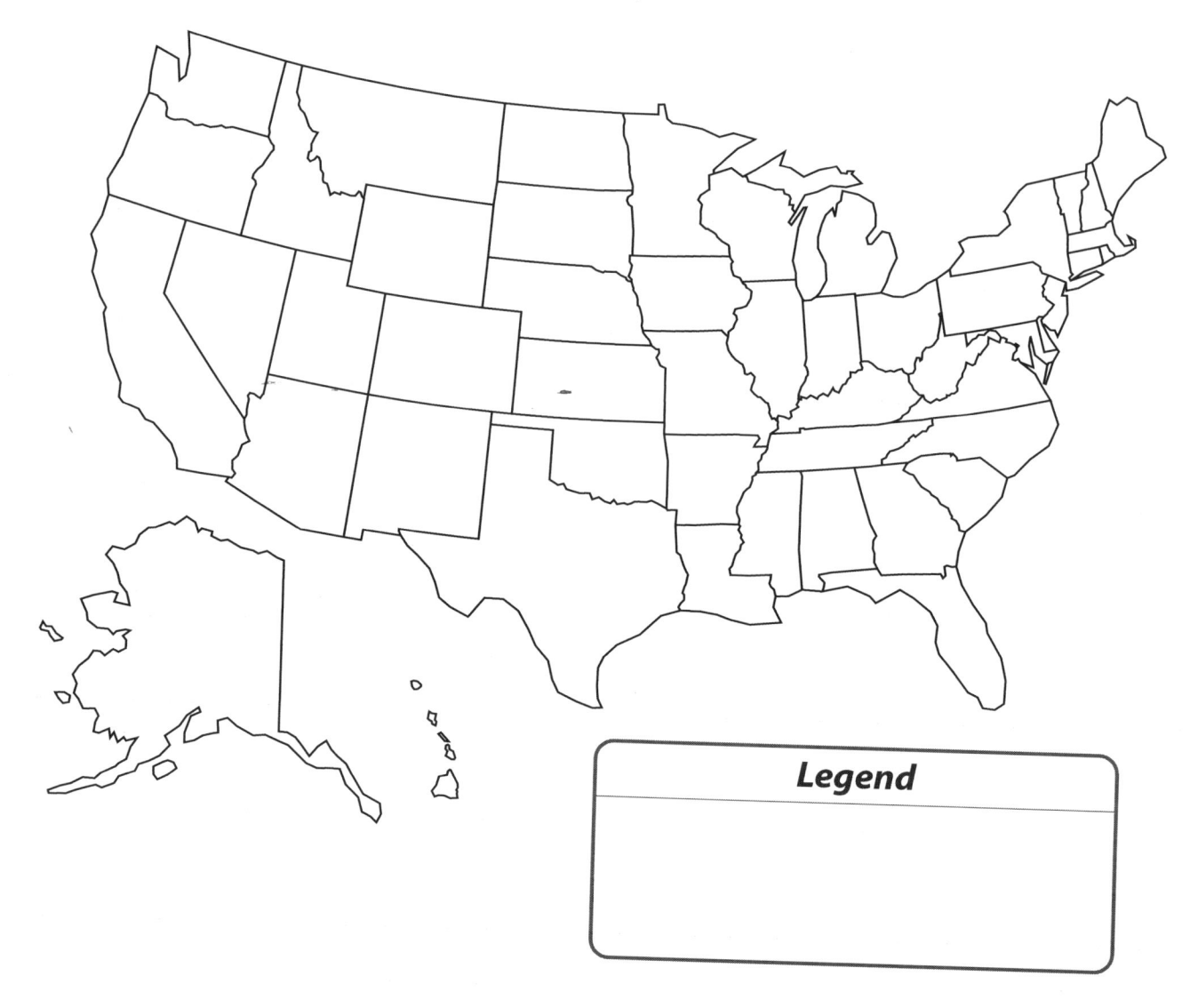

Legend

22.3 My Story in a Map

Social Studies

Name: _____ Date: _____

Point of View

Perspectives can change over time. Use what you learned to comple the activity below.

Read the situation below. Then think about the two perspectives th appear over time about the same event. Write each perspective in boxes below.

Situation

Before America became its own country, it belonged to the Britis The British made the Americans pay high taxes to them for the items they needed. The people living in America were thankful for the supplies that the British gave them.

Over time, the people in America did not like being controlled by t British. They were tired of paying taxes. This was because they d not have a say in the decisions the British government made. The wanted to be independent of Britain. This way they would not ha to pay the taxes and follow the British rules.

Perspective #1	Perspective #2

23.1 Perspective of Time

2. The reason I do not want to do this chore:

3. The benefits of doing this chore:

4. What different perspective can I have about the chore if I do it every day?

23.2 Perspective of Experience

Social Studies

Name: _____ Date: _____

My Problem and Solution

Every problem can have multiple solutions. Someone's perspective on the problem will depend on how they experience the situation. Use what you have learned to complete the activity below.

Think of a time when you had a problem with someone. Maybe you are dealing with a problem with a family member or friend right now! Write your problem in the box below.

1. Problem:

next page →

23.3 Recognizing Perspectives for Problem-Solving

2. Why do you feel this way about your problem?

3. Ask the other person about their perspective, or think about it from the other point of view. What is the other perspective?

4. Think about both perspectives. What could be the solution to your problem?

23.3 Recognizing Perspectives for Problem-Solving

Social Studies

Name: _____ Date: _____

Fill Your Needs

Answer each question in a complete sentence. Think of answers that are true for your life.

1. What is one way that your need for food is filled?

2. What is one way that your need for water is filled?

3. What is one way that your need for clothes is filled?

4. What is one way that your need for shelter is filled?

Social Studies

Name: _____ Date: _____

Shopping Spree

Pretend that you have $10.00 to spend at the store. First, choose two items that fill your needs. Then you can spend the rest of the money on your wants! Write the name of each item and its price in the correct box on the next page. You do not need to spend all of your money, but you cannot spend more than you have. Fill in the blanks for questions 2 and 3 to show how much money, if any, you have left.

1. Circle one item to fill your need for food and one item to fill your need for water. Then, circle three items that you want. Make sure you do not spend more than $10.00.

lemonade $1.00	gummy candy $1.00	banana $1.00	pickle $1.00
sidewalk chalk $2.00	chips $2.00	milk $2.00	glow sticks $2.00
soda $2.00	adventure book $3.00	chicken sandwich $3.00	cake pops $3.00
nail polish $3.00	toy car $4.00	flower headband $4.00	building block set $5.00

next page ➡

24.2 Wants

22

Need for food	Need for water
Item: _____	Item: _____
Price: _____	Price: _____

Want 1	Want 2	Want 3
Item: _____	Item: _____	Item: _____
Price: _____	Price: _____	Price: _____

2. I spent this much money: _____

3. I have this much money left: _____

Social Studies

Name: _____ Date: _____

Bag Sort

Each bag below holds something that was bought at the store. Decide if each bag holds a want or a need. Color the wants pink. Color the needs green.

- pants
- apple
- necklace
- soccer ball
- stuffed animal
- water bottle
- video game
- chocolate
- shoes
- coloring book

24.3 Comparing Wants and Needs

Social Studies

Name: _____   Date: _____

Needs and Wants

Tyler made a Venn diagram to compare and contrast needs and wants. He made four mistakes while he was working. Rewrite the Venn diagram to correct Tyler's mistakes. Your Venn diagram should contain only the items that Tyler wrote. Do not add any of your own items. Then answer the question below your diagram.

needs | **both** | **wants**

- video game
- water
- jacket
- steak
- puzzle
- mansion
- bike
- a safe place to sleep

next page →

25

24.4 Project: Needs and Wants

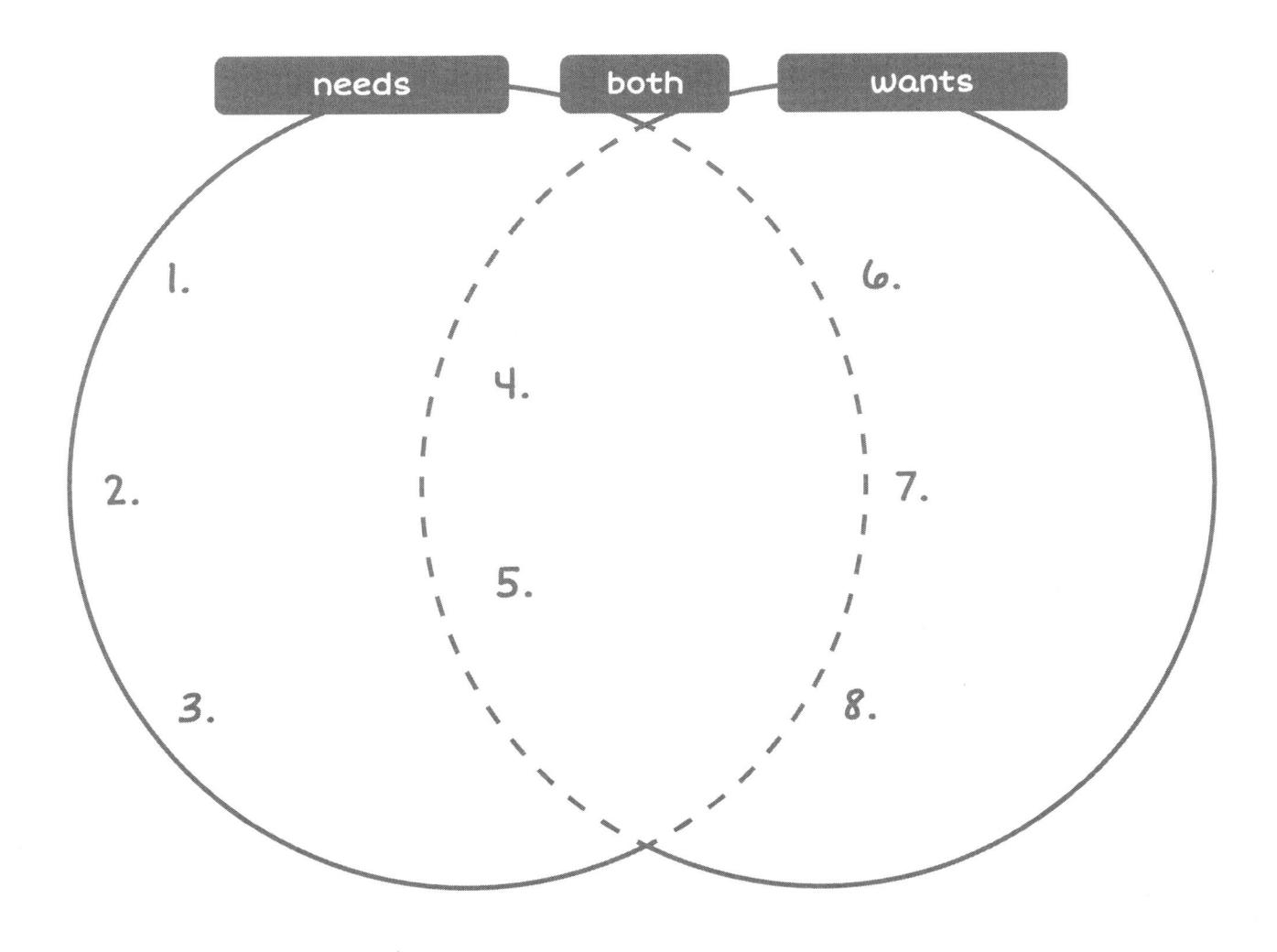

needs | both | wants

1.
2.
3.
4.
5.
6.
7.
8.

9. Choose one item from the "both" category. Explain why it is both a need and a want.

24.4 Project: Needs and Wants

Social Studies

Name: _____ Date: _____

Sorting the Goods

Now it is your turn to look at different goods and decide what types of goods they are. Read through the list of goods in the box. Write the name of each good in the box where it belongs.

List of Goods

- streetlights
- theme park membership
- airplane tickets
- libraries
- beaches
- timber from trees
- tickets for a show
- gym membership
- TV streaming services
- fish for fishing
- lunch at a restaurant
- wildflowers for picking

Public Goods

Club Goods

Common Goods

Private Goods

27

25.1 Goods

Name: _____ Date: _____

Draw the Service

Draw an example of a business service, a personal service, and a social service in each of the boxes below. On the lines below each drawing, describe the service you drew.

Business Service

Personal Service

Social Service

25.2 Services

28

Social Studies

Name: _____ Date: _____

Categorize Goods and Services

Read the words in each circle below. If the words describe a good, color the circle blue. If the words describe a service, color the circle yellow.

| goods | blue | | services | Yellow |

- picking wildflowers
- fishing for fish
- doctor's visit
- public beaches
- security guard
- books
- technology support
- hairdresser
- housecleaner
- firefighter
- jewelry
- fruits and vegetables

29   25.3 Categorizing Goods and Services

Social Studies

Name: _____ Date: _____

Money Earned

It is your turn to draw and write about your needs and wants. Then write about how you could earn money to pay for your wants and needs.

1. Draw a picture of something you NEED. Write what you need and explain why you need it.

next page

26.1 Income = Money to Pay for Wants and Needs

30

2. Draw a picture of something you WANT. Write what you want and explain why you want it.

3. How can you earn money, and what can you use your earned money for?

26.1 Income = Money to Pay for Wants and Needs

Name: _____ Date: _____

My Job

We all have needs and wants. To purchase your needs and wants, you need money. You can earn money from your job. Use what you know about work, value, and income to answer the questions below.

1. What do you want to be when you grow up? Draw a picture in the box. Label it.

26.2 Work = Value and Income

2. What will be the value of the job you chose?

3. Explain some of the goods and services that you will be able to buy with the money you earn from your job.

Social Studies

Name: _____ Date: _____

True or False?

People earn income from their jobs. The amount workers are paid is determined by their education, experience, and skills. Read each scenario below. Use what you learned in the lesson to decide if it is true or false.

1. Mindy has always wanted to become a teacher. She graduated college and got a job teaching second grade. She worked full-time and went back to school to get her master's degree in education. Once she received her master's degree, she made the same amount of money as when she first started teaching. True or false? Circle the correct answer below.

    True   False

2. Phil became a construction worker when he graduated high school. He worked full-time and attended different training programs to become certified to drive different machines. Once he received his certifications, he made more money than when he started. True or false? Circle the correct answer below.

    True   False

next page

26.3 Job Skills = Bigger Paycheck

3. Sally graduated college and got a job teaching high school. She worked full-time and went back to school to get a reading specialist certification. Once she received her certificate, she made less money than when she started. True or false? Circle the correct answer below.

            True   False

4. Sammy was a babysitter in her neighborhood. She started babysitting when she was 12 years old. When she became a teenager, she decided to take courses to better prepare herself for emergencies. She took CPR and first aid courses. Once she completed those courses, she made more money babysitting each child. True or false? Circle the correct answer below.

            True   False

5. Joey joined the U.S. Army when he graduated high school. He chose a career as a tanker, and he trained other students. He continued his training while being an instructor. He has been on active duty for 18 months and has earned a higher rank. He makes more money now than when he first started in the Army. True or false? Circle the correct answer below.

           True   False

Social Studies

Name: _____ Date: _____

Producers

Read each scenario below. Each one tells a story about the role of a producer. Once you read the story, write how the producer fulfilled their role in that situation.

1. A clothing store was selling a particular brand of T-shirt twice as fast as other brands. The producer started making the T-shirts at a faster rate to keep up with the demand. How did the producer fulfill his role?

   _____
   _____
   _____
   _____
   _____
   _____
   _____
   _____

2. A farmer sprays fertilizer on his crops every year. This helps his crops grow big to supply the local grocery stores. But this chemical also lands on the neighbors' houses and yards. This is not good for the environment. A company created a product that helps crops grow and is safe for the environment. How did the producer fulfill her role?

   _____
   _____
   _____
   _____
   _____
   _____
   _____
   _____

next page →

27.1 Producers

3. The line to get into the ice-skating rink was very long. A staff member had to stamp everyone's ticket on the way in. A company invented a product that stamps tickets automatically. Now there is no line at the skating rink. How did the producer fulfill his role?

Social Studies

Name: _____ Date: _____

I Am a Consumer

Consumers purchase goods and services every day. Use what you learned in the lesson to complete the activity below.

1. How are you a consumer in your local community? Draw a picture in the box of you at your favorite store, buying a product, or paying for a service.

2. Write two sentences on the lines below explaining why your role as a consumer is very important to your community.

_____
_____
_____
_____

27.2 Consumers

Social Studies

Name: _____ Date: _____

Complete the Cycle

Consumers and producers rely on each other. Consumers purchase goods and services in the local community, and producers supply those goods and services. Use what you learned in the lesson to complete the activity below.

Part A: Fill in the blanks on the circle graph to explain the relationship between producers and consumers. You can review the slideshow in the lesson to help you.

1. _____

2. _____

4. _____

3. _____

next page

27.3 Interdependence

Part B: Read the situation, and fill in the blank.

5. If the producer runs out of a product, then the consumer...

27.3 Interdependence

Social Studies

Name: _____ Date: _____

My Production Process

Every product you see at a store has gone through a process. Producers start the production process so that consumers have goods to buy. Use what you learned in your research to answer the questions below to help you create your timeline.

1. What is the first step in the process of creating a bicycle?
   _____
   _____
   _____
   _____
   _____
   _____

2. How do workers help produce a bicycle for consumers?
   _____
   _____
   _____
   _____
   _____
   _____

next page

27.4 Project: My Production Process

3. What is the role of the producer?

4. How do consumers help the businesses?

27.4 Project: My Production Process

5. Now it is time to build your timeline. Use your answers above to create a timeline that explains the process of how a bicycle goes from the producer to the consumer. You can draw or create your timeline in the space below, on a poster board, in a slideshow presentation, in a flip-book, or any other way you choose. When you have completed your timeline, submit it to your teacher.

Social Studies

Name: _____ Date: _____

Orange Scarcity

Reread the article entitled "Florida Oranges" found in the lesson. What do you think the effect of orange scarcity might be on each group of people below? Write two sentences to explain your ideas for each group.

Ask yourself these questions:

- What will happen to this group because of the scarcity of oranges?
- What might this group have to do because of the scarcity of oranges?

1. Florida orange farmers:

_____
_____
_____
_____
_____

2. Grocery store owners:

_____
_____
_____
_____
_____

next page ➡

28.2 Limited Resources

3. Families who buy orange juice:

4. School cafeteria workers:

Social Studies

Name: _____ Date: _____

Strawberry Scarcity

Read the realistic fiction story below. Then answer the questions.

> Most of the strawberries eaten in the United States are grown in Mexico. Over the last few months, there has been a drought where the strawberry fields are located. Many strawberry plants have died after going a long time with too little water. American grocery stores cannot get as many strawberries as they need for all the people who want to buy them. Luna is one of those people.
>
> Luna loves strawberries! She eats strawberries with her cereal in the morning. She packs strawberries to eat with her lunch. She even cuts up strawberries to put on her ice cream for dessert! She has really missed eating strawberries during the scarcity.
>
> One day, Luna found a store that had strawberries for sale! She was so excited! She bought six cartons of strawberries. She put them in her freezer so that she can keep them as long as the strawberry scarcity lasts. Now Luna can enjoy her favorite treat until more strawberries can be grown.

1. What caused the strawberry scarcity?

   _____
   _____
   _____
   _____

next page

28.3 Choices When Resources Are Limited

2. What choice did Luna make because of the scarcity?

3. In your opinion, did Luna make a good choice? Explain why you have this opinion.

4. What is another choice that Luna could have made?

Social Studies

Name: _____ Date: _____

A Picture of Farming

Draw a picture to show what farming was like in the past and what it is like today. Then write two sentences to explain each one.

Farming in the Past	Farming Today

29.1 America's Farmers: Long Ago and Today

Social Studies

Name: _____ Date: _____

Growing Weather

Pretend you are a farmer growing corn in Iowa. Which types of weather are good for your crops? Read each leaf. Color the leaf green if the weather is good for crops. Color the leaf yellow if the weather is bad for crops.

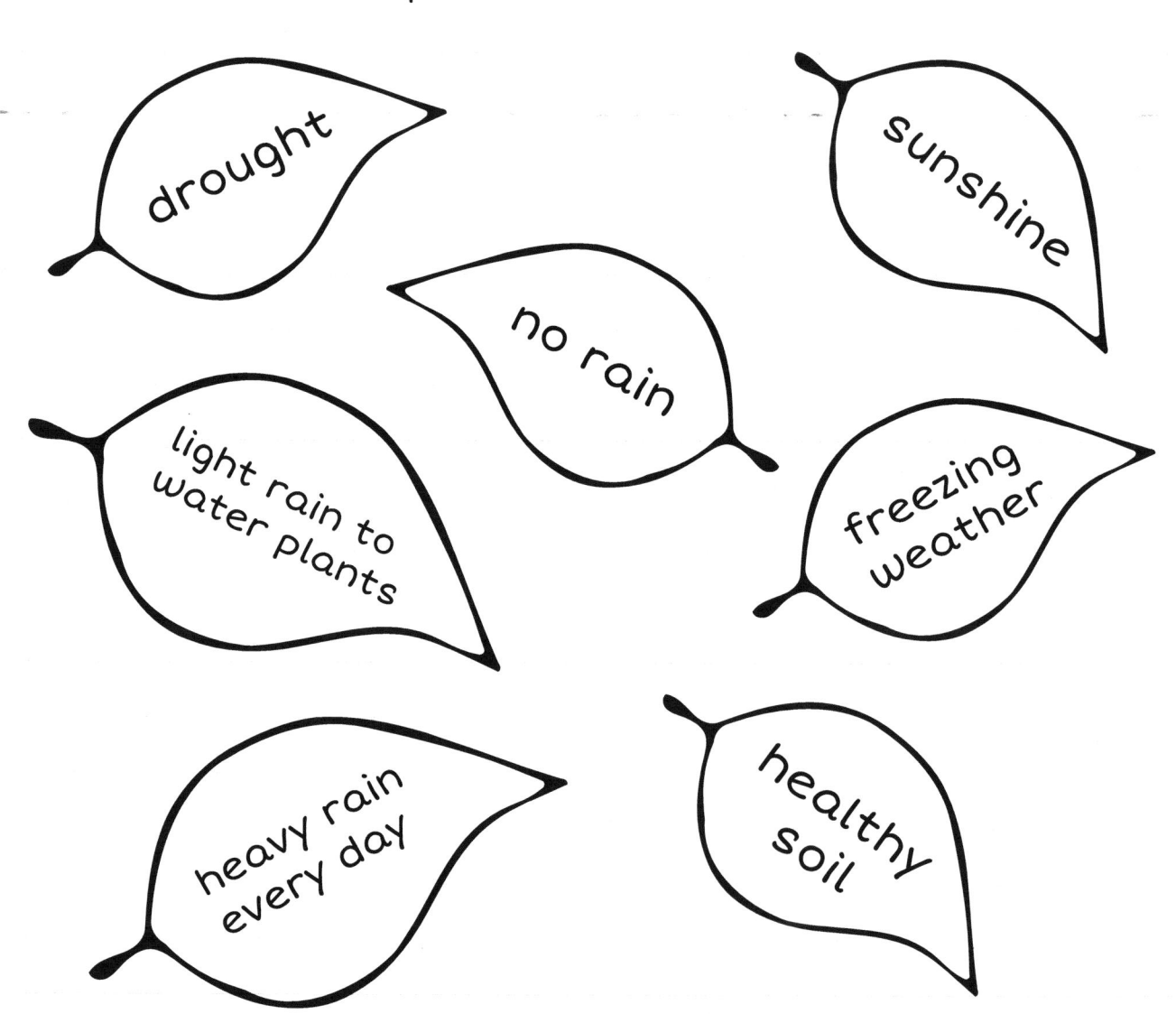

- drought
- sunshine
- no rain
- light rain to water plants
- freezing weather
- heavy rain every day
- healthy soil

Social Studies

Name: _____ Date: _____

Highlighting Supply

Read each story. Then highlight or underline the words in the story that show the supply. Remember, supply is how much of a good or service is available. Use the example in the box below to help you.

> Phillip is at the carnival. He won a prize at the ring toss! There are <u>a hundred stuffed animals for him to choose from</u>!

1. Michael is going to the barbershop with his dad. Some of the barbers are out sick today. There is only one person working at the barbershop. Michael has to wait a long time to get his hair cut.

2. Maya and her mom are going to bake a cake today! They need to buy a bag of sugar. At the grocery store, the sugar aisle is almost empty! They buy the last bag of sugar.

3. Haley is having a party for St. Patrick's Day. The store has a lot of green decorations to choose from! Haley buys a green tablecloth and chocolate coins.

next page ➡

30.1 Supply

4. Eli wants to buy fireworks for the Fourth of July. He waited too long to buy his fireworks, however. The fireworks are almost all sold out!

5. Cora wants to buy a chocolate donut as a treat. The trays at the donut shop are full of different donuts for her to pick from! Cora chooses a chocolate donut with blue sprinkles.

6. Does story number 5 have a high supply or low supply?

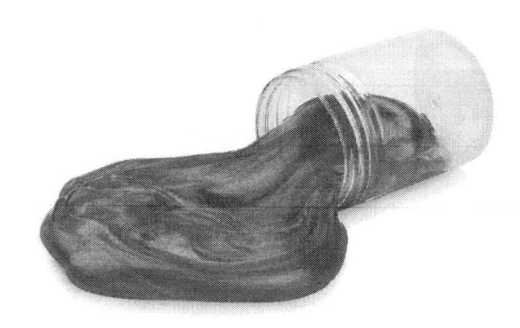

Social Studies

Name: _____ Date: _____

Coloring Demand

Read the story in each box. Decide if it is an example of high demand or low demand. Remember, demand is high when many people want a good or service. Demand is low when only a few people want a good or service. Color each box using the key below.

| high demand | Green | | low demand | Pink |

The comic book shop has 15 comic books that have a rip on the cover. No one wants to buy them!	Ms. Donor's class is having a pizza party. Most of her students want cheese pizza.	Only one person bought tickets to Maria's violin recital.
In the winter, very few people buy bathing suits.	Tony's pet store cannot find anyone who wants to buy the green tree snake.	Stores sell many American flags before the Fourth of July.
The store is full of people who want to buy flowers on Valentine's Day.	A new dress has been shared online. Now thousands of people want to buy it!	The grocery store has sold out of apple juice because so many people are buying it.

30.2 Demand

Social Studies

Name: _____ Date: _____

Changing Supply

Read the scenarios below about supply and demand at different stores. Decide what change the store should make and write your answer on the line.

1. The Clothing Store

A clothing store has 100 hats to sell. People are buying belts but not hats. What should happen next?

_____
_____
_____
_____

2. The Donut Shop

A donut shop has 20 plain donuts and 50 chocolate donuts. Most people are buying plain donuts. What should happen next?

_____
_____
_____
_____

next page

30.4 Project: Changing Supply

3. The Pet Shop

A pet shop has 15 betta fish for sale. Many people have been coming in to buy them. What should happen next?

4. The Bakery

The bakery has 50 bags of hamburger buns to sell. People are buying hot dog buns but not hamburger buns. What should happen next?

30.4 Project: Changing Supply

Social Studies

Name: _____ Date: _____

Saving My Money

In this lesson, you have learned that you can save a lot of money over time. Remember, saving money helps us buy what we need in an emergency or buy something that we cannot afford right away. Use what you have learned to calculate your savings below.

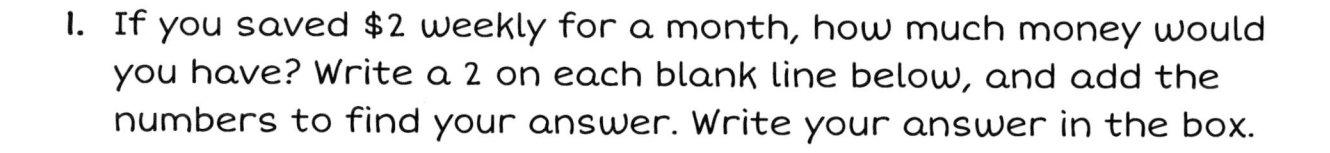

1. If you saved $2 weekly for a month, how much money would you have? Write a 2 on each blank line below, and add the numbers to find your answer. Write your answer in the box.

    $____ + $____ + $____ + $____ = $ ☐

2. If you saved that amount for three months, how much money would you have? Write the amount you saved for one month on each blank line below. Add to find the total. Write the total in the box.

    $____ + $____ + $____ = $ ☐

next page

55
31.1 Saving

3. Write the amount you saved in one month on the six blank lines below. Add up the savings. How much did you save in six months? Write the amount in the box.

$____ + $____ + $____ + $____ + $____ + $____ = $ ☐

4. What would you choose to do with your savings? Write your answer on the lines below.

31.1 Saving

Social Studies

Name: _____ Date: _____

My Spending

Saving money will help you when you have an emergency or when you want to buy something that you cannot afford right away. You will always have choices about what to spend your money on. Use what you have learned to calculate your savings below.

1. Imagine you have earned $50. Draw a picture of something you would buy with your earnings. Label your picture and include how much it costs.

$

next page

57

31.2 Spending

2. In this box, write how much money you would have left. This is the amount you are saving.

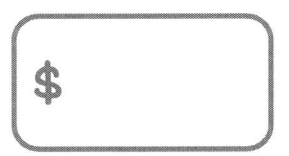

$ ☐

3. Write one sentence explaining why it benefits you to save some of your money.

_____

_____

_____

_____

_____

31.2 Spending

Social Studies

Name: _____ Date: _____

My Choices

Now you can practice making choices about money. Read the scenario below. Then choose what you will do with your money.

> You babysat while Mr. and Mrs. Smith went out to dinner and a movie. You earned $10 an hour. You watched the children from 5:00 p.m. to 10:00 p.m., so you made $50.

1. What will you do with the $50 you just earned from babysitting? Write what you will do on the lines below.

   _____
   _____
   _____
   _____

2. Did you choose to spend, save, or earn more? Circle your answer below.

   Earn   **Save**   **Spend**

3. Why did you select your answer?

   _____
   _____
   _____
   _____
   _____

Social Studies

Name: _____ Date: _____

Money-Saving Behaviors

Money-saving behaviors help you make good decisions about your money. Read the scenario below. Then use what you have learned to answer the questions below.

> Jimmy loves helping his grandma. His grandma pays him $10 each Saturday for cutting the grass in her yard. He puts his earnings in his piggy bank each time. By the end of the month, he has $40.

REACH GOAL
STICK TO IT
GET TO WORK
MAKE PLAN
SET GOAL

1. Does Jimmy show money-saving behaviors? How does he show this? Write your answer on the lines below.

   _____
   _____
   _____
   _____

2. If you were Jimmy, what would you do with the $40 you earned this month? Write your answers on the lines below.

   _____
   _____
   _____
   _____

32.1 How to Save

Social Studies

Name: _____ Date: _____

My Savings

Use what you have learned to answer the questions below.

1. Draw a picture of a big purchase you would like to make. Label it.

2. Find out how much it costs. Write the amount below.

_____

_____

3. Now create a plan for how you can save that money and how long it will take you.

_____

_____

_____

_____

next page

32.2 Saving for a Big Purchase

4. Use the boxes below to show each step of your plan until you have reached the amount you need. Add more boxes if you need to!

5. How long will it take you to save enough money to buy what you want?

_____

_____

32.2 Saving for a Big Purchase

Social Studies

Name: _____ Date: _____

Why Save?

Read the situations in the boxes below. Decide what the person or family can do in each situation to save the money they need. Write your answers in the empty Action boxes.

Situation	Action
1. In September, the Smith family decided to go to Disney World next summer. They need to save money in order to buy all the tickets. What should they do?	
2. Ben wants to save money in case he has a future emergency. What should he do?	

next page →

63

32.3 Bank Savings Account

Situation	Action
3. The Jones family would like to install a backyard pool this summer. What should they do?	
4. Jenny sees a new dress she wants to buy at the store. She does not have enough money to buy the dress. What should she do?	

32.3 Bank Savings Account

Social Studies

Name: _____ Date: _____

Local Business

Think of a local business in your town. Draw a picture of the business. Then write the name of the business. Explain what type of good or service it offers.

Business name: _____

Social Studies

Name: _____ Date: _____

Good Business Owners

Choose **one** of the character traits listed. Write a paragraph to explain why business owners need that character trait. Think about the tasks or responsibilities the trait helps business owners do.

    creative   organized   good leader

33.2 Bosses and Employees

Social Studies

Name: _____ Date: _____

Closed for Business

Think about each group of people below. What is one way that each group is affected when a business closes in the community? Draw a picture of what happens to a business owner, a worker, and a customer when their business closes. Write a sentence to explain each of your drawings.

1. Business Owners

2. Workers / Employees

3. Customers

33.3 Business Closes

Social Studies

Name: _____ Date: _____

What Would My Product Cost?

In this lesson, you saw all the parts it takes to get products onto store shelves. You also learned how to figure out the suggested retail price of an item. Use what you learned to answer the questions below.

1. The manufacturer is making sleeping bags. The supplies cost $15. The labor costs $9. The shipping cost is $5. The desired profit for each sleeping bag is $5. What will the suggested retail price be? Write the answer on the line below.

   _____

   _____

2. Think of a product. Guess what each part costs. Then calculate your suggested retail price. Write your answers below.

   Your product _____

   Supply costs _____

   Labor costs _____

   Shipping costs _____

   Desired profit _____

   Suggested retail price _____

34.1 Prices

Social Studies

Name: _____ Date: _____

Which Price Is Correct?

When there is competition, businesses have to make changes to sell their products. Read the scenarios below. Use what you learned in the lesson to answer the questions.

1. The ice cream shop sells an ice cream cone for $4. In the winter, it is hard for the ice cream shop to make money. The hot chocolate stand next door attracts many customers, however. The ice cream shop needs to change its price to get more customers. Circle the price below that would help the ice cream shop make money in the winter.

    $5 $3

2. There are two car wash businesses on the same street. They both get the same number of customers each day, and they charge the same price. It is $8 for one car wash. One business wants to make more profit, so it starts a sale. Each car wash is half off every Saturday. Circle the cost of a car wash at this business on Saturdays.

    $10 $4

3. Benny just opened a cookie stand on his street. He is selling cookies for $3 each. He notices that his neighbor is selling the exact same product at the same price. Because of the competition, Benny makes a change. He advertises that his cookies are now $1 off. Circle the correct price below to help him make money even with competition.

    $4 $2

next page

34.2 Competition

4. Besides changing the price of a product, what can businesses do so they can still make money even with competition?

Social Studies

Name: _____ Date: _____

Scarcity vs. Price

Read the text in each box below. If the price of the item goes up, color the box blue. If the price stays the same or goes down, color the box red. Then answer the question below.

1. There are a lot of fireworks left at the store after July 4th celebrations.

2. It is the beginning of summer. Stores have beach supplies out to sell.

3. There is a shortage of bottled water. Only a few stores have cases of water.

4. The store made a mistake and ordered too many sunglasses.

5. The milk supplier is delayed due to a snowstorm. No milk is being delivered.

6. What is the law that states that if the item we want is limited, its value goes up? Write your answer on the lines below.

_____ _____

_____ _____

71

34.3 Scarcity

Name: _____   Date: _____

Trading Patterns

People trade for many reasons. These reasons follow certain patterns. Read each scenario below, and write the reason that the trade would happen. You will use each pattern of trade in the word bank once.

Word Bank:	technology	scale of production
	demand	climate	resources

1. Lucy uses stencils to make bookmarks. She can make 25 bookmarks a day. What is the reason someone would trade with Lucy?

   _____

   _____

2. Skylar's mom makes the best brownies. His friends always ask for his mom's brownies. What is the reason someone would trade with Skylar?

   _____

   _____

3. Jen has figured out a way to use an app on her laptop to control the robot she made at school. What is the reason someone would trade with Jen?

   _____

   _____

next page ➡

35.1 Trading

4. Paul has lots of carrots in his garden, but he did not grow any tomatoes this year. Anthony's garden is full of tomatoes. What is the reason Paul and Anthony would trade?

_____

- -

_____

5. Lily's favorite fruit is watermelon. But Lily cannot eat watermelon during the winter because it is too cold for them to grow. Her best friend moved to a place where it is warm year-round, and she is coming for a visit soon! What is the reason Lily would trade with her friend?

_____

- -

_____

Name: _____ Date: _____

Worldwide Trade

The United States gets some of its resources from other countries by trading. Use what you learned in the lesson to complete the activity. Read the text in each box and match it with the best trade option.

1. The climate in the U.S. allows many oranges to grow but not many cacao beans.

2. Canada has abundant forests, but it does not have many modern machines and technology.

3. The Middle East has many places to drill for oil, but it does not have the equipment to build airplanes for transportation.

4. Mexico has a lot of farms where avocados are grown, but the country grows very little rice.

5. Japan is a major exporter of cars, but it does not produce a lot of plastics.

The United States has a lot of factories that make airplane parts, but most of its land is not suitable for drilling for oil.

Africa grows lots of cacao beans, but it does not grow many oranges.

India has lots of rice fields, but it does not grow many avocados.

China has a large population and many buildings but not many forests. China does have many factories and uses advanced technology.

The United States exports plastics to other countries and gets imported cars in return.

35.2 International Exchange of Goods

Social Studies

Name: _____ Date: _____

Is That True?

Every country trades goods and services with other countries. Not every country has the same resources. Climate, labor costs, and production technology all play a part in each country's imports and exports. Read each sentence below. Using what you learned in the lesson, decide if each statement is true or false. Circle the correct answer.

1. The United States only exports goods to other countries.

    True   False

2. International trade happens when countries export and import goods and services to and from other countries.

    True   False

3. International trade involves just one country.

    True   False

4. Countries export goods and services because other countries are not able to produce those goods and services.

    True   False

5. Some examples of services that the U.S. exports are computer services, travel services, and business and financial services.

    True   False

75   35.3 International Exchange of Services

Social Studies

Name: _____ Date: _____

Finding Problems

Practice identifying the problems by completing the activity below.

1. Read the sentence in each box. If the box contains a problem, color the box yellow. If the box does not contain a problem, color the box pink. When you are done, use the letters from the yellow boxes to spell a synonym for the word "problem."

1. I forgot to study for my vocabulary test today. **T**	2. I cleaned my room before dinner. **A**	3. I got an F on my spelling quiz. **R**
4. I helped my little sister put on her shoes. **D**	5. I got an A on my math test. **S**	6. I did not take out the trash, but I told my mom that I did. **O**
7. I lost my library book. **U**	8. I turned my book report in on time. **V**	9. I did not turn in my classwork yesterday. **B**
10. I did an extra credit project for reading. **G**	11. I forgot to feed my pet fish. **L**	12. I dropped my homework in a puddle. **E**

2. What is another word that means problem? The first letter has been done for you.

   T __ __ __ __ __ __ __

36.1 Step 1: Identify the Problem

Social Studies

Name: _____ Date: _____

Identifying Options

Read about Ariel's problem and one of the options she has thought of to solve her problem. Write one pro and one con for her option. Then write to explain whether you think this option is an advantage or a disadvantage.

> Ariel wants to go to the movies with her friends next weekend. A movie ticket costs $12. Ariel has not earned enough allowance money to pay for her ticket! This is a problem because she will not be able to go out with her friends. Ariel thinks about her options.
>
> **Option:** Ariel can ask her parents for more chores this week so she can earn more money.

1. What is one pro and one con for this option?

Pro	Con

next page

36.2 Step 2: Identify the Options

2. Do you think this option is an advantage or a disadvantage? Explain your reason.

36.2 Step 2: Identify the Options

Social Studies

Name: _____ Date: _____

Ariel's Solution

Read about Ariel's problem and options. Then decide whether Ariel chose the right solution.

> Ariel wants to go to the movies with her friends next weekend. A movie ticket costs $12. Ariel has not earned enough allowance money to pay for her ticket! This is a problem because she will not be able to go out with her friends. Ariel thinks about her options.
>
> **Option 1:** Ariel can choose not to go to the movies.
>
> **Option 2:** Ariel can do extra chores this week to earn more money.
>
> **Option 3:** Ariel can ask one of her friends to buy her movie ticket.
>
> Ariel chose option number two. She did extra chores to earn more money so she could go to the movies.

Do you think Ariel made the right choice? Give two reasons to support your answer. Write your answers in complete sentences.

_____
_____
_____
_____
_____
_____

79   36.3 Step 3: Identify and Evaluate the Solution

Social Studies

Name: _____ Date: _____

My Problem and Solution

Think of a real problem that you have in your life and complete the activities below.

1. Draw your problem, and write two sentences to describe it on the lines.

Problem

next page ➡

36.4 Project: My Problem and Solution

80

2. Think of three possible solutions for your problem. Draw a solution in each box, and write two sentences to describe each solution.

Solution Option 1

Solution Option 2

next page

81

36.4 Project: My Problem and Solution

Solution Option 3

3. Select the best option and explain why you chose it.

   a. Circle your choice below.
      I chose option number   1   2   3

   b. I chose this option because . . .

36.4 Project: My Problem and Solution

Cutout Worksheets

Name: _____   Date: _____

World Artifacts Map

Cut out the pictures of artifacts below along the dotted lines. Find the spot on the map that shows where each artifact was found. Glue the picture in the correct box.

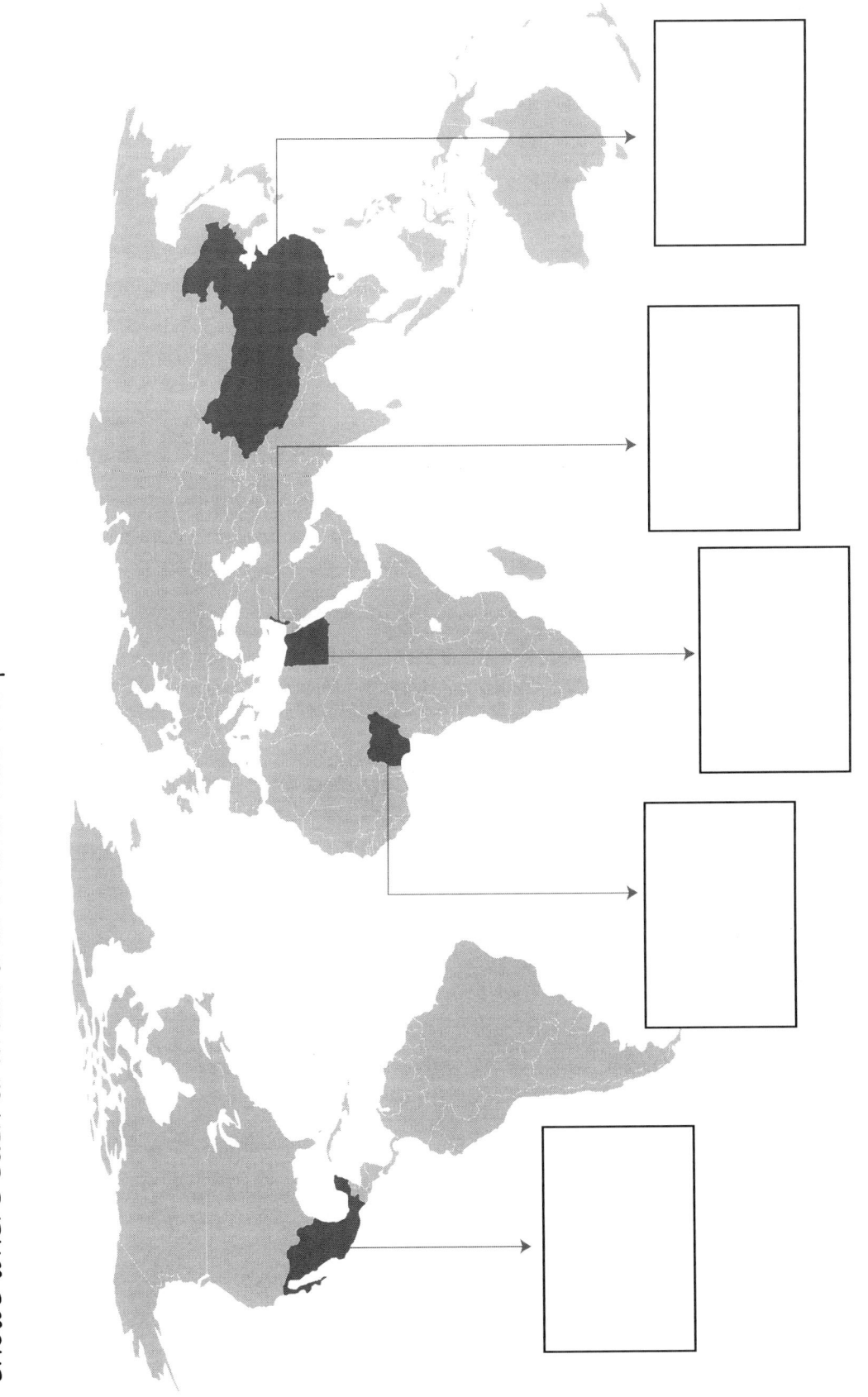

19.3 World Historical Artifacts

84

19.3 World Historical Artifacts

Rosetta Stone | Dead Sea Scrolls | Terracotta Army | Olmec heads | Benin ivory mask

Social Studies

Name: _____ Date: _____

Fun With Recreation

Recreational activities are fun things we do together. You have learned how technology has changed the way we spend time together. In this activity, you will sort activities into two groups and then identify how technology has changed the activities.

1. Look at the images on the last page of this worksheet. Do they represent something from the past or the present? Cut out the images along the dotted lines. Glue them into the correct boxes for past or present.

2. Then write about how technology has changed each recreational activity.

Past

Theater

Present

Theater

How has technology changed theater?

_____
_____
_____
_____

next page →

20.3 Recreation: Past and Present

88

Past	Present
Art	Art

How has technology changed art?

___

Past	Present
Toys	Toys

How has technology changed toys?

___

next page

20.3 Recreation: Past and Present

20.3 Recreation: Past and Present

Social Studies

Name: _____ Date: _____

American Inventors

Look at the pictures below. Each one represents an inventor or invention. Cut out the pictures of inventions along the dotted lines. Paste each invention next to the inventor who created it.

Emily Warren Roebling

Henry Ford

Maria Beasley

next page →

21.2 Inventors

Thomas Jennings

Swati Mohan

21.2 Inventors

Name: _____   Date: _____

Garrett Morgan's Timeline

A timeline can tell us the order of events in a person's life. Write or draw the important events in Garrett Morgan's life on the tabs below. Cut out the tabs along the dotted lines, and glue them in the correct order on the timeline. You should include events from the very beginning of his life to the end. Review the story in the lesson to add more details to your timeline.

21.3 Creating a Timeline

96

Social Studies

Name: _____ Date: _____

Sorting Resources

Cut out the boxes at the bottom of the page along the dotted lines. Decide what kind of resource each item is. Glue each word in the box that lists the correct type of resource. The boxes will not all have the same number of answers inside them.

LAND	LABOR

CAPITAL	ENTERPRISE

Amazon®   coal   chef

money   loan   Walmart®

Burger King®

28.1 Resources

Name: _____ Date: _____

The Life of Potato Chips

Cut out the images along the dotted lines. Think about the steps in the food manufacturing process. How can those steps be used to make and sell potato chips? Glue the images in the correct order in the boxes below.

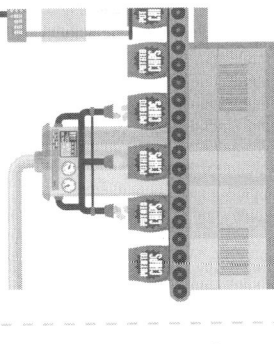

1	2	3	4	5

Consumers buy bags of potato chips at the grocery store.

Food manufacturers use potatoes to make bags of potato chips.

Potatoes are grown on a farm.

Consumers eat potato chips with their lunch.

Food distributors transport potato chips from the factory to the store.

29.2 Getting Food: Long Ago and Today

100

Social Studies

Name: _____ Date: _____

On Sale

Cut out the stories below along the dotted lines. Read each story. Then decide if the good should be on sale. If the good should be on sale, glue the story in the sale sign box. If it should not be on sale, do not glue it in the box!

SALE

There is a low supply of water bottles, but many people need to buy them.	The store has a lot of candy the day after Halloween, but no one wants to buy it.	The store has a lot of plain donuts, but everyone wants to buy chocolate donuts.
The store still has hundreds of bathing suits in the winter, but no one wants to buy them.	Many people want to buy the newest phone, but there are not enough for everyone.	The store's supply of nail polish is too high. It has more nail polish than people want to buy.

30.3 Connection

© 2023 by Accelerate Education
Visit us on the Web at: www.accelerate.education
ISBN: 978-1-63916-162-1